NEVER MIND

THE TOFFEES

2

Another Ultimate
EVERTON

QUIZ BOOK

GAVIN BUCKLAND
FOREWORD BY IAN SNODIN

The History Press

First published 2017

The History Press
The Mill, Brimscombe Port
Stroud, Gloucestershire, GL5 2QG
www.thehistorypress.co.uk

British Library Cataloguing in Publication Data.
A catalogue record for this book is available from the British Library.

ISBN 978 0 7509 8428 7

Typesetting and origination by The History Press
Printed and bound by CPI Group (UK) Ltd, Croydon, CR0 4YY

Contents

Foreword

When I joined Everton in 1987, I realised pretty quickly that most Blues know their history and enjoyed being tested on it. This has been proved to me many times in my years on local radio in the city, and I can confirm the Blues are far more knowledgeable than their Red counterparts! I also enjoy being quizzed on my football and sporting knowledge and this is put to the test when I face my former Liverpool rival Gary Gillespie in our weekly challenge on our popular BBC Radio Merseyside show *Snods and Diz*.

Therefore I was pleased to be asked to contribute the foreword to *Never Mind the Toffees 2*. There's plenty of stuff in here that even I wasn't aware of, like when I scored in the game that had the lowest top-flight attendance in history! Having said that, hopefully all the questions give you a chance of an answer so I hope you enjoy the book.

Ian Snodin
2017

Introduction

Welcome to *Never Mind the Toffees 2*, the follow-up to – you will never guess – the *Never Mind the Toffees* quiz book first published in 2013. With more than 300 new Everton questions, as sequels go this is hopefully more *Godfather 2* than *Jaws 2*.

To say that events at Goodison following the publication of the first book have been interesting would be an understatement. After a hugely promising beginning, Roberto Martinez's reign ended in 2016 and his replacement, Ronald Koeman had an excellent first campaign. But the most exciting development was the arrival of Farhad Moshiri at the club in February 2016 – the businessman providing the funds that will hopefully give Everton a golden future to match our glorious past. Not surprisingly, there are more than a few questions to test your knowledge of the club over the past four years. Elsewhere, the book has made no effort whatsoever to change a winning formula: plenty of themed rounds and several that will test your general knowledge of all things in Toffeeland.

Hopefully you find the questions to be like a Reid, Bracewell, Sheedy and Steven midfield – plenty of flair and originality but providing tough opposition when needed. Most should give an opportunity to have a decent guess if you do not know the answer. Speaking of former players, my great thanks go to a favourite of mine, the title-winning Blue and Everton ambassador, Ian Snodin, for providing the foreword. From personal experience, Snods knows his stuff.

Finally, I hope you are up for the challenge and don't get too frustrated when the question about the right-back in our 1891 title-winning team crops up … or is that one for *Never Mind the Toffees 3*?

Gavin Buckland, 2017

A quick note on the content: things can move quickly in the football world, so it's worth pointing out that the questions and answers are factually correct as at the end of the 2016/17 campaign.

About the Author

GAVIN BUCKLAND has written several books on Everton, contributes to their matchday programme, magazine and website, and is the official Club statistician. He lives in Liverpool.

Round 1

Warming Up

The quiz equivalent of a pre-season friendly – a bit of light work to get rid of the rust before the serious business begins.

1 Where did Everton play their home games before moving to Goodison in 1892?

2 Who did David Moyes replace as manager in 2002?

3 From which club did Everton sign Romelu Lukaku for a club record fee of £28 million in 2014?

4 Who left Goodison in 2016, having made a club record 354 Premier League appearances in ten years at Everton?

5 How many times did Howard Kendall win the league title with Everton, as both a player and a manager?

6   Which club legend joined for £150,000 from Bury in
    1981 and played his last game sixteen years later?

7   Who was Everton manager between Howard Kendall's
    first two stints as boss?

8   Who played his last game for Everton in 2006 before
    promotion to first-team coach in February 2014?

9   Who succeeded Phil Neville as club captain in 2013?

10 Where was Everton's training complex before they
    relocated to Finch Farm in 2007?

11 Who was signed for a club record fee of £15 million
    from Standard Liege in 2008?

Under Martinez: Part I

Unfortunately the Spaniard has come and gone; however, in his three seasons at the helm there were some memorable moments which are recalled here.

1 Who scored his first Everton goal in Roberto Martinez's opening game as manager against Norwich in August 2013?

2 Whose final goal for the club was the winner, just 27 seconds after coming on as a substitute, in the 2–1 victory over Hull City in October 2013?

3   Which then League One side did we beat in both the League Cup and FA Cup in the 2013/14 season?

4   Which Everton player controversially nominated himself as penalty-taker and then saw his spot-kick strike the post in a game against West Brom at Goodison in January 2015?

5   Which Martinez signing scored his first Everton goal at Hull City in the final game of the 2013/14 season?

6   Who were our opponents in November 2015 when both teams dramatically scored in second-half injury time in a 3–3 draw?

7   Oumar Niasse was the second player Martinez bought from a Russian club as Everton manager – who did

the Spaniard purchase from Spartak Moscow for £1.5 million in January 2014?

8   In the 3–1 win at Burnley in October 2014, who became the first Everton player wearing the number 5 jersey to score twice in a league game for twenty-eight years?

9   Which side knocked us out of the Europa League in the Round of 16 in March 2015, 6–4 on aggregate?

10   In the 2016 FA Cup semi-final at Wembley, who became the fourth player to appear both for and against Everton on the ground?

11   Which former MK Dons player made his Everton debut at West Ham in May 2015?

Round

3

Opening Days

No matter how bad the summer has been, it is always guaranteed to be cracking the flags in August when the seasons starts, so here's a few on the opening day to brighten up things.

1   An Everton player has only once scored the first goal of the Premier League season: which winger did so after 10 minutes of a 2–0 win at Southampton in August 1993?

2   Which club has had four spells in the top-flight, with the first game in three of them being against Everton – on the opening day in the 1982/83, 2006/07 and 2015/16 seasons?

3   Which team put 6 goals past Everton at Goodison on the opening day of the 2009/10 campaign?

4   Which newly signed international missed a penalty on his debut against Aston Villa on the opening day of the 1998/99 campaign?

5   Everton's opening day game in three successive seasons from 2013/14 onwards all ended in the same result – what was it?

6   Signed for a club record £8.6 million, who scored on his debut on the opening day of the 2006/07 season?

7   Which member of our 1984/85 championship-winning squad played his last game for the club, strangely on the opening day in August 1986, before moving to Watford?

8 Who netted his only Everton goal when opening the scoring at Leicester on the first day of the 2014/15 season?

9 Who were the brothers who scored against Everton at Goodison on the opening day of the season fifteen years apart – one for Norwich in 1979 and the other for Aston Villa in 1994?

10 Between 2008 and 2016, Everton won only one game on their opening day of the Premier League season, against which team in 2012?

11 Which goalkeeper made his Everton debut against Spurs on the opening day in 2002, having faced the Toffees for Arsenal in the last game of the previous season?

Round

4

A Mixed Bag
of Toffees

Variety is the spice of Everton life, so here is the first of a
number of general knowledge rounds that will test your
knowledge of events over the years, including Everton's
greatest strikers, 1970s goalkeepers and, er, a certain
tracksuit ...

1   Which Toffees' player had all seven letters in
    EVERTON in the twelve that made up his first name
    and surname?
2   Which Everton player famously tried to take a
    penalty whilst wearing his tracksuit top in the

penalty shoot-out against Sunderland at Goodison in
November 1998?

3 Which striker did Everton sign from Leicester City for
a fee in excess of £1 million in the summer of 1989?

4 Two Everton players have been capped for Australia –
Tim Cahill and who else with three appearances in 2009?

5 Who overtook Brian Labone's club record for an
outfielder by playing for Everton in sixteen different
seasons?

6 Who scored 97 goals for the club in 369 games, the
most by any player who never scored a hat-trick?

7 Against which club did Graeme Sharp score in 10
different games – the most by an Everton player against
any club in the post-war era?

8   Which club recorded their first league victory over the Toffees at the twenty-second attempt in January 2016?

9   Which player scored just 2 goals in his Everton career – the first of which was against Scunthorpe in the League Cup in September 1997?

10 On which ground have Everton played the most FA Cup semi-finals?

11 Which goalkeeper, signed for a record fee of £80,000 from Huddersfield in the summer of 1972, later played for the Toffees in the 1977 League Cup final?

Round

5

Toffees in
the FA Cup

With five final victories, plus countless other memorable
campaigns and games, the FA Cup forms an essential part
of the fabric of Everton's past and present, providing a rich
source of material to test you on. No putting out your second
string to answer the questions either!

I   Which side defeated us after a marathon penalty
     shoot-out that featured 20 spot-kicks in the third
     round in January 2015?

2   Which overseas player scored 3 FA Cup goals, the last
    of which was in his final club appearance in January
    2014?

3   Which then League One team knocked Everton out
    at Goodison at the third round stage in 2008, before
    the Toffees gained revenge five years later with a fifth-
    round replay victory?

4   Which side have we played on most occasions in the FA
    Cup, a competition-record 23 games in total?

5   Which manager took charge of Everton in 11 FA Cup
    games at Goodison, winning the first 10 before drawing
    his last home contest?

6   Everton suffered a shock 2–1 loss at Shrewsbury in the
    third round in 2003, but which Toffees' legend was in
    charge of the victors?

7   Which defender made his final Everton appearance in
    the 1989 FA Cup final against Liverpool?

8   Against Birmingham City in January 2000, who became
    the first Everton player to score two penalties in the
    same FA Cup game?

9   Which famous Everton FA Cup goalscorer said, 'I made
    contact [with the ball] with my head and there was no
    bodily contact'?

10 Who refused to celebrate after scoring the winning
    goal against Millwall at Goodison in the third round in
    January 2006?

11 Everton suffered their biggest home FA Cup defeat for
    48 years in January 2007, when which side won 4–1 at
    Goodison in the third round?

Round
6

Goodison Goings-On

Everton celebrate 125 years at the Grand Old Lady in 2017, making it the home of so many happy memories for those of a Blue persuasion. This round tests your knowledge of some famous events at the ground, with a few strange moments captured here too.

1   What Goodison Park first occurred following Zlatan Ibrahimović's goal for Manchester United in December 2016?

2   Why did the encounter against West Ham make headlines in December 2000?

3   Why was there an unusual 5-minute hold-up in the
     game against Manchester City in February 2012?

4   In October 2014, which club did we face for the 100th
     time in home league games, the first occasion this
     landmark had been reached in domestic football?

5   Which referee controversially disallowed Don
     Hutchison's goal in the Goodison derby of April 2000,
     after Liverpool goalkeeper Sander Westerveld's
     clearance struck him and rebounded in?

6   Everton won a penalty shoot-out at the ground for the
     first time in 45 years in October 2015. Who were our
     opponents in the League Cup?

7   Which side have we scored 8, 7 and 6 goals against at
     Goodison in separate league games since 1970?

8   What was missing in the first half of Everton's 1–1 draw against Birmingham City at the ground in March 2011?

9   Whose strike from outside the box against Larissa in the UEFA Cup in October 2007, after a flowing team move, is regarded as one of the best goals scored at the ground?

10 Who was an unexpected guest in the stands for the home draw against Reading in January 2007?

11 'My instructions are that at the end of the game there will be nobody on the pitch, and that means nobody' were the words of which participant in one of the Merseyside derby's most memorable incidents?

Premier League: The Noughties and Beyond

Despite a slow start and some mega-rich rivals, the Premier League has largely been good for the Toffees and it is hoped that the arrival of Farhad Moshiri (in 2016) will herald a new golden age. Your millennium knowledge is put to the test here.

1   Which team did we lose to for the first time in 16 Premier League games in a 3–2 defeat at Goodison in March 2016, after we led 2–0?

2   Whose late goal for us secured a famous 4–4 draw
    with Manchester United at Old Trafford in April 2012?

3   Which Toffees' cult hero scored a single Premier
    League goal for the club in the 2–0 victory over
    Chelsea at Goodison in February 2012?

4   Everton defeated which team 2–0 in May 2005 to
    effectively seal a place in the Champions League
    qualifiers?

5   Which Everton player was voted the Premier League
    Player of the Month for February 2009, one of only
    seven to win the award whilst at the club?

6   At which ground did Everton record a Premier League
    victory in December 2013 for the first time in twenty-
    one years?

7   Yakubu Aiyegbeni scored one Premier League hat-trick
    for us, against which side in December 2007?

8   Who was our top Premier League scorer, for the
    only time, in the 2009/10 season with 13 goals in 33
    appearances?

9   Which Toffees' outfielder played in every minute of a
    Premier League campaign on two occasions, in 2010/11
    and 2012/13?

10 After Nick Barmby in February 2000, who was the
    next Everton player to score a Premier League away
    hat-trick?

11 Who in May 2009 became the first overseas player to
    make 200 Premier League appearances for Everton?

8

Loan Stars

One of the features of the modern game are the numbers of players on loan from other clubs, and Everton have been no exception. Some have been great successes and others not so, one even having the name on his shirt spelt incorrectly!

1   Which overseas midfield player had two loan spells at the club, in the 2006/07 and 2007/08 campaigns, but never signed a permanent deal?
2   Which Italian defender played 8 Premier League games during the 2005/06 season, when on loan from Roma?
3   Which loan player from Arsenal made his Everton debut against Wigan in January 2010?

4   Which player did Everton take on loan from the North American Soccer League in 2003?

5   When Duncan Ferguson arrived on loan from Rangers in 1994, which Ibrox team-mate was also part of the deal but only played 5 Premier League games for the Toffees?

6   Who returned to Everton for a second spell in August 2007, when on loan from Celtic?

7   Everton took Gerard Deulofeu on loan from Barcelona in 2013, but which player had we earlier taken on loan from their bitter rivals, Real Madrid?

8   Which player came on loan from Chelsea in the summer of 2014, making just five Premier League starts?

9 Which future England international did we take on loan from Sporting Lisbon in January 2011, although he never played for the first-team?

10 Kevin Campbell was playing football in which country before he came on loan in March 1999?

11 Which player returned to Goodison for a second loan spell in three seasons in December 2011?

Round

9

Blues Opponents

It takes two to tango, so every memorable Everton performance has also been a day to forget for our rivals on the pitch, and sadly vice versa! These questions will test your knowledge of those who have faced us over the years.

1 Who were our opponents when Everton scored 6 goals in a Sunday fixture for the first time?
2 Which is the only club to record 100 or more victories against Everton in first-team games?
3 During the 2015/16 campaign, which team did Everton defeat in the Premier League on Boxing Day before

waiting six weeks for their next Premier League victory, strangely against the same side?

4   David Moyes faced which team thirty-two times as Everton manager, a club record for an Everton boss?

5   Everton have faced which city's two clubs in penalty shoot-outs in the League Cup, losing one in 2000 and winning the other in 2004?

6   Wayne Rooney famously ended a 51-year wait for a league win at which club in November 2002?

7   Which manager won Premier League games at Goodison with three different clubs in five seasons from 2011/12 to 2015/16 inclusive?

8   At the end of the 2016/17 season, Everton had gone 441 minutes without conceding a league goal at which

Premier League away ground, the second longest such sequence in our history?

9 Which club have we faced five times in the FA Cup since 1963, losing all five ties – two in the third round, once in the fifth round, a quarter-final and a semi-final?

10 Which club did we defeat three times in FA Cup ties in the 1980s: 1981, the trophy-winning year of 1984 and in 1987?

11 Which club's then English record of 34 league games unbeaten did Everton end with a 3–2 home win in August 1969?

Round

10

Another Mixed Bag of Toffees

The same drill. A pot pourri of questions ranging from transfers across Stanley Park to unbeaten runs on a particular day of the week.

1 Who is the only player to have been transferred from Liverpool to Everton for a seven-figure fee?
2 Which side did Everton prevent from reaching a fourth successive FA Cup final with a 2–0 win at Goodison in the third round in January 1981?
3 Who is the only Everton player to score post-war derby match goals at the Gwladys Street and Park End

at Goodison, and the Kop and Anfield Road ends across the Park?

4   Duncan Ferguson scored with his final touch as an Everton player in May 2006, but which Scottish team-mate repeated the feat at Goodison exactly twelve months later?

5   'Everyone went on about it, but it was straight at me' – who is the Everton player speaking, and what was he talking about?

6   Apart from Andy Gray, which other player in our 1984 FA Cup final winning team had not appeared against Liverpool in the League Cup final at Wembley two months before?

7   Prior to Ashley Williams in 2016, who (ten years earlier) had been the last Everton player capped by Wales?

8   Whose only goal for Everton came in the 3–0 victory over Manchester United in April 2015?

9   From which club did Everton sign goalkeepers Gordon West in the 1960s and George Wood in the 1970s?

10   On which day of the week did Everton not lose in a 17-game sequence from November 2008 until a 4–3 defeat by Stoke in December 2015?

11   Which overseas striker made his only Everton appearance in the third round of the FA Cup against Dagenham and Redbridge in January 2016?

Round

11

The Merseyside Derby

This is the most played fixture in the English game, with the two teams having squared off more than 220 times in all competitions. It has been the game with everything over the years: comical own goals, mass brawls, multiple red cards and a streaker – and that was only the October 1979 clash! Your Mersey knowledge is put to the test here, just make sure you get more questions right than your Anfield counterpart does.

1   Who is the only Everton keeper to save a penalty in a league derby game?

2   Which player scored our final derby goal in the old
    first division in December 1991, and then our first goal
    against Liverpool in the newly formed Premier League
    twelve months later?

3   We defeated Liverpool for the first time in five years
    at Goodison in December 2004. Who was the only
    player to appear for us in that game and in our previous
    victory, at Anfield in September 1999?

4   Players from which country featured on both sides
    for the first time in the Goodison derby of December
    2016?

5   Who made his only derby appearance for Everton in
    January 1995, thus becoming the first player to appear
    in Premier League derbies for both teams?

6   In the controversial 2–1 defeat at Goodison in October 2007, Everton opened the scoring thanks to an own goal from which Liverpool player?

7   Which Irishman became the youngest Everton player to start in a derby game at Goodison in April 1997, being 17 years 207 days old?

8   In the two Anfield league derbies staged in 1999, which Everton player scored in the first and was sent off in the second?

9   Of all the players who have played for both clubs, who has made the most derby appearances – 27 in total: 7 for Everton and 20 for our rivals?

10 Who is the only substitute keeper from the bench used by Everton in derby match history?

11 Which was the first overseas country to provide two different Everton goal-scorers in the same derby game?

Overseas Blues

Another feature of the modern game is the growing number of overseas players. Many have enhanced the Premier League and Everton, like other clubs, have had their share of the good and, perhaps, not so clever.

1 In 2016 Romelu Lukaku became Everton's highest scoring overseas player – whose record did he break?
2 Who was the first Everton player capped by France when with the club?
3 Who scored after just 3 minutes 54 seconds of his Everton debut against Swansea in the FA Cup in February 2014 but made only one further appearance, against Hull, on the final day of the season?

4 After joining Everton in January 2016, who played for his country at that year's Euros before making his first-team debut for the club?

5 Which future Everton player was born in Poznań, Poland in December 1973?

6 Which overseas goalkeeper was on the bench for every Premier League game in the 2010/11 and 2011/12 seasons but did not make a single league appearance in either season?

7 Who won 44 caps in his Everton career from 2000 to 2004, the most with the club for a country in Continental Europe?

8   Against which side did Magaye Gueye and Idrissa Gana Gueye both score their first Everton goal?

9   Which European country has had two players appear for Everton, both of whom played in goal for the Blues?

10 Which Everton player memorably said on social media: 'I'm retiring from the France team. It was a wonderful experience and after a record of 0 caps it's time to say goodbye and focus on my club'?

11 Which overseas player has uniquely played for both clubs in the Merseyside derby in the same season?

Round

13

Debuts to Remember (and Forget!)

Wearing the Blue shirt for the first time is surely a career highlight for Everton players. First experiences have ranged from the truly memorable, to the bizarre and the disastrous. All are covered here.

1   Later to be a key player of the successful mid-1980s squad, who gave away a crucial penalty after making his debut as a substitute in a 2–1 home defeat to Sunderland in November 1981?

2   Which goalkeeper made one appearance for Everton in
    a 1–0 defeat to BATE Borisov in the Europa League in
    December 2009?

3   Who played on both sides of Stanley Park during
    his career in the 1970s and scored for us on his first
    appearances in the league, FA Cup, League Cup, the
    derby and in Europe?

4   Later to skipper the club, who netted on his debut
    against Newcastle on the opening day of the season in
    August 1996?

5   Whose one and only first-team appearance saw him
    infamously sent off after 37 minutes of the Merseyside
    derby at Goodison in November 1982?

6 Who made his Everton debut in the 2–1 home win over Arsenal in December 2016, his sliced clearance being part of an amazing final minute?

7 Which full-back memorably made his debut in the 6–1 win over Arsenal at Goodison in November 1985?

8 Which overseas player's disastrous first touch on his debut lead to Chelsea's final goal in their 6–3 win at Goodison in August 2014?

9 Which goalkeeper made his Everton debut after Richard Wright injured himself in the warm-up at Stamford Bridge in February 2006?

10 Signed from Manchester City, which 32-year-old made his Everton debut against Liverpool in the 1986 Charity Shield?

11 Who scored the third fastest debut goal in Everton post-war history against Manchester City in January 2017?

Round 14

The 1970s

The 1970s have been described as the 'decade that style forgot'. While that may be true, it is worth remembering that our 1970 championship-winning team was one of the most elegant in Everton history. The questions here look at later events, when even a trophy drought could not totally ruin a fondly remembered decade.

1   Which former player took over from Harry Catterick as manager in May 1973?
2   In which year did Everton buy Bob Latchford for a British record fee of £350,000 from Birmingham City?
3   In August 1978, Latchford scored five times as which lower-league club were on the receiving end of an 8–0

drubbing in the League Cup at Goodison, on the most recent occasion that the Toffees have scored 8 in a game?

4   Who scored for Everton in three successive Merseyside derby games during the decade?

5   What happened, perhaps appropriately on Bonfire Night, for the second and last time in an Everton game at Derby County in November 1977?

6   Who made the most first-team appearances for Everton during the decade, a player whose own goal at Anfield in October 1979 delighted one Toffees' supporter, who won £40 on him to score the first goal?

7   The Toffees played 58 games in the 1976/77 season, reaching the League Cup final and FA Cup semi-final.

Which centre-half played in all those matches in his last season for Everton, creating a then club record for most domestic appearances in a single campaign?

8   Bought for a club-record fee of £180,000 from Aberdeen in December 1972, which striker then missed a penalty on his debut against Spurs?

9   Which club legend made his final appearance in the League Cup defeat at Southampton in September 1971?

10 Everton made their first purchase from an overseas club in December 1976, paying £200,000 for the services of which player?

11 A 22-game unbeaten run came to an abrupt end when which team beat us 6–2 at Goodison on Boxing Day 1977?

Round

15

Comeback Kings

We all know the feeling. Everton trail 2–0, the opposition are on fire and there's no way back. But we nick a goal and all of a sudden it's a different game. The questions here cover those memorable occasions when the Toffees have snatched victory from the jaws of defeat.

1   In August 2015 Everton defeated which lower division side 5–3 in the League Cup, having trailed 2–0 at half-time?

2   In the following month, which team did the Toffees beat 3–2 to record their first away league win from 2 goals down for thirty years?

3   Whose 2 late goals at Goodison sealed a memorable 2–1 win over Southampton in February 2003?

4   Everton have won only one derby game from behind in the post-war era; who scored the winner in December 1992?

5   In the 3–2 victory at West Ham in September 2013, after trailing twice, who became the first Everton player since Alan Ball to score a debut winner?

6   Who were our opponents in February 2011 when the lead changed hands three times in our first 5–3 win at Goodison for seventy-three years?

7   Which club did we defeat 7–2 on aggregate, after trailing in both legs, in the Europa League Round of 32 in February 2015?

8   From 1–0 down, Everton recorded their first Premier
    League win under Ronald Koeman at West Brom in
    August 2016. Whose rare header gave the Blues a 2–1
    victory?

9   In lifting the European Cup Winners' Cup in 1985, the
    Toffees needed only to come from behind once to win
    a game: who were our opponents?

10 In the second game of the 2004/05 season, we
    recorded a crucial 3–1 away victory at Crystal Palace,
    after trailing 1–0 in a match cruelly described as 'the
    earliest six-pointer in Premier League history'. But
    who scored 2 goals in that game for the only time in his
    Everton career?

11 We defeated West Ham 2–1 away from 1–0 down in
    May 2015: whose equaliser was the forty-fourth and
    final Premier League goal of his Everton career?

Round
16

Toffees for the Three Lions

More than sixty Everton players have appeared for England, collectively winning over 500 caps for the national team. Here are eleven questions on those who have starred for the Three Lions.

1   Who played twice for England whilst at Everton –
    against Spain and Sweden in 2011?
2   Who is the only Everton player to appear for
    England in the qualifiers for two different World Cup
    tournaments?

3   Which Everton player won his only England cap against
     Japan at Wembley in June 1995?

4   Which Everton defender won his only England cap
     against Spain in Sven-Göran Eriksson's first game in
     charge in February 2001?

5   Which Toffees player made his England debut as a
     substitute in the 3–0 win against Peru at Wembley in
     May 2014?

6   Who was the only Everton player to appear for England
     at the 2000 European Championships, coming off the
     bench twice?

7   Who, when playing against Northern Ireland in
     February 1985, became the first Everton player capped
     by England for six years?

8 Which player's England record whilst at Goodison was 9 goals scored in 11 internationals?

9 A member of our 1995 FA Cup winning side, he made four England appearances during his time at Goodison from 1996 to 1997. Who is he?

10 Which then Everton player won his 12th and final England cap against Russia at the 1988 European Championships?

11 Which then Everton striker won six England caps from 2006 to 2007 but failed to score for his country?

Round

17

Howard Kendall: The 1990s Management Years

The great man returned to Goodison in 1990 but former glories failed to follow. There was enough, though, to get eleven half-decent questions.

1   Which non-league team did Everton defeat 1–0 at Goodison in the fourth round of the FA Cup in January 1991?

2   In 1991, which was the last club Howard faced as Everton manager at Wembley?

3   Howard later managed them, but the first game in his second spell was a goalless draw against which team in November 1990?

4   Which member of our 1995 FA Cup-winning team holds the record for the longest time between scoring Premier League goals (after netting for Everton in May 1993 his next strike was for Wigan thirteen years later)?

5   Howard paid a fee of £1.5 million for the services of which striker in November 1991?

6   For which former Liverpool player did Howard pay a fee of £1.1 million to Sheffield United in February 1998?

7 Who was our leading scorer in the 1991/92 season with 20 goals in all competitions?

8 Who did Howard sign from Manchester City for £1.1 million in the summer of 1991, a local player the club had previously released more than a decade before?

9 At which ground in 1993 did Howard joke: 'Yes, I was hit by eggs, but I don't want to make a big deal about it, you would have thought that Dave Watson, with all his experience, would have known better than to sit next to me here'?

10 For the only time in Premier League history, two 17-year-olds scored for the same team in a game during our 2–2 draw with Arsenal in September 1997 – name either Everton player?

11 Howard gave a debut to which Everton player at Spurs in April 1992, who scored as a substitute before making more than 300 Premier League appearances for the club?

Round

18

Under Martinez: Part II

Here are eleven more questions on the Spaniard's managerial spell at Goodison, which will hopefully evoke some decent memories.

1   The Spaniard's first Premier League victory as Everton manager came over Jose Mourinho's Chelsea in September 2013. Who was in our team that day, having played against the Stamford Bridge side in Mourinho's previous Premier League defeat in September 2007?

2   Everton had not lost a home league game in the
    calendar year of 2013 until Boxing Day, when which
    side won 1–0, with Tim Howard sent off?

3   In the FA Cup win over QPR in January 2014 who, in
    his final game for the club, became only the second
    Everton player ever to miss a penalty when on a hat-
    trick?

4   Against Newcastle in December 2014, who became the
    first player to score for Everton wearing the famous
    number 9 shirt since Landon Donovan in 2010?

5   Who became our then most expensive defender at
    £9.5 million when bought by Roberto Martinez in his
    time at Goodison?

6 Which Everton player was included in the PFA Team of the Season for the first time for the 2013/14 campaign?

7 In 2014/15, who became the first Everton player to score in the first three league games of a season since Alex Young in 1962?

8 Who scored in both of our victories over Manchester United in the Premier League at Goodison in April 2014 (2–0) and April 2015 (3–0)?

9 Which team were awarded four penalties against Everton in the Premier League during the 2015/16 season?

10 Which Irish international, who made 5 Premier League appearances for the Toffees, moved to Blackburn for a fee of £1.5 million on transfer deadline day in September 2014?

11 Whose last-minute equaliser earned Everton a 1–1 draw at Anfield in September 2014?

Round

19

Tell Me Ma, Me Ma...We're Going to Wembley

Which is something we have done many times, since our first visit in 1933 when we defeated Manchester City 3–0 in the FA Cup final. Some memorable games at both stadiums in that time are recalled here.

1   Only one penalty has been awarded in an Everton game at Wembley – who took it?
2   Who in the 1970s and '80s was the first player to appear for and against Everton at Wembley?

3   Who replaced the injured Phil Jagielka in the starting line-up for the 2009 FA Cup final against Chelsea?

4   Who was the only Manchester United player to appear against us at Wembley in the 1995 FA Cup final and the semi-final fourteen years later?

5   Who captained Everton in the 1977 League Cup final against Aston Villa, in our first appearance under the twin towers for nine years?

6   Who made his first Everton appearance in the Charity Shield against Manchester United at Wembley in August 1985, and his last against Liverpool in the FA Cup final there nine months later?

7   Who made a club record 11 appearances for Everton at Wembley?

8   Who is the only Everton player to score in two different finals at Wembley?

9   Which former Everton striker played for Blackburn against the Toffees at Wembley in the 1995 Charity Shield?

10   Who is the youngest player to appear for Everton at Wembley, at the age of 18 years 39 days in the 2009 FA Cup semi-final against Manchester United?

11   Two opposition players have scored own goals in Everton games at Wembley – Bruce Grobbelaar in the 1984 Charity Shield and who else?

The Early Bath

For a player, there is nothing worse than being sent off and letting down your team-mates, manager and supporters. Some players – mentioning no names – have been attracted to the red card more than others …

1   Who is the only player sent off whilst playing for and against Everton: twice for us and for Sunderland at Goodison in May 2001?

2   Who was red-carded twice for Everton in the 2015/16 season – at Swansea and at home to West Ham?

3   Against Chelsea in December 2002, who became the first Everton player to be sent off at Goodison Park in league games on three occasions?

4   In September 2004, referee Steve Bennett dismissed which Everton player for a second bookable offence, for lifting his shirt over his head after scoring?

5   Which player was sent off against Chelsea twice, in the Premier League in February 2015 and the FA Cup twelve months later?

6   Which current Premier League side has had fourteen players sent off against Everton in all competitions – the most by any club against the Toffees?

7   Against Sheffield Wednesday in February 1993, who became the first player sent off three times playing for Everton?

8   Apart from Duncan Ferguson, who is the only player
    sent off on more than three occasions for us, being
    red-carded four times between 1999 and 2003?

9   Who is the only Everton player sent off twice in the
    Merseyside derby, at Goodison in December 2005 and
    October 2007?

10 Whose infamous red card given by referee Martin
    Atkinson in the Goodison derby of October 2011 was
    later rescinded?

11 Which self-proclaimed 'hard man' was sent off against
    Everton at Goodison in two successive seasons, in
    1987/88 and 1988/89?

Round

21

Yet Another Mixed Bag of Toffees

This round does exactly what it says on the tin, with some general knowledge questions on the Blues, including which Everton player is better at doing something than Lionel Messi ...?

1 Who won 86 caps in his England career, and scored once in seven Everton appearances in early 1993?
2 Real Sociedad's Xabi Prieto has scored 6 league goals (more than any other player) against teams managed

by Jose Mourinho. But who scored 5 goals against him at Everton to be next highest, immediately ahead of Lionel Messi?

3   In his final season at the club, which cult hero came on as a substitute in the 1984 League Cup final replay at Maine Road?

4   Who scored the most goals in all competitions for Everton during the 1990s – 78 in total?

5   Which player was Everton's joint top-scorer in the Premier League in 2001/02 with 6 goals, and the highest in the following campaign with 11?

6   Who is Everton's all-time top-scoring full-back from open play?

7   Who left the club in the summer of 2013 for a reported fee of £5 million, having not been on the losing side in

the 24 games in which he had scored for Everton, a club record at the time?

8   In 2000, Mark and Stephen were the first names of the last pair of players to appear in the same Everton team with the same surname – what is it?

9   Who scored 82 Premier League goals in his career (of which 45 came with Everton), the highest total in the Premier League by an Englishman never capped for his country?

10 Who joined Everton from Hearts for a reported fee of £42,000 in 1960?

11 Who has taken spot-kicks for Everton in a record five different penalty shoot-outs, the first being against Fiorentina in 2008?

Round

22

Wearing the Armband

One of the great privileges for the select few is captaining the mighty Blues. Some, like Brian Labone or Kevin Ratcliffe, did so on many occasions, but for others it was only a temporary honour.

1   Who skippered the team for the first time in the FA Cup game at Arsenal in March 2014?
2   Who led Everton to 16 wins in his 18 matches as skipper after wearing the armband for the first time in 2009?

3   Who captained the Toffees for the only time in the Europa League game against Krasnodar at Goodison in December 2014?

4   Who was club captain immediately before Kevin Ratcliffe?

5   In the game against Newcastle in February 1998 who became the first overseas player to captain Everton?

6   Who wore the captain's armband in our first ever Premier League game, against Sheffield Wednesday in August 1992?

7   Who is the only player to score a Premier League hat-trick whilst captaining the team?

8   Whose only campaign as club skipper was the 2005/06 season?

9   Who captained for the first time against Yeovil in the League Cup in August 2016, making him the youngest Toffees' skipper for thirty-three years?

10 And then who skippered the side for the first time in the 2–0 home defeat to Norwich in the same competition four weeks later?

11 Which Scot captained Everton for the first time in just his 15th Premier League game at Charlton in November 1998?

Blues Brothers in Arms

Key players in the revival under David Moyes, Tim Cahill and Mikel Arteta brought a bit of Aussie grit and determination and a touch of Iberian flair to Goodison for a combined fee of less than £5 million. Hopefully these questions will provide equally good value.

On Mikel Arteta

1   Everton signed Mikel from which Spanish team, initially on loan, in January 2005?
2   His first goal came via a free-kick in a 4–0 home victory over which side in April 2005?

3   The Spaniard missed a year of first-team action after
    sustaining a cruciate ligament injury at which ground in
    February 2009?

4   Mikel scored 2 goals in a Premier League game at
    Goodison on one occasion, in a 5–1 home victory in
    March 2010. Who were our opponents?

5   Against which side did Mikel score his final goal for
    Everton, a last minute penalty securing a 1–0 victory,
    days before his transfer to Arsenal in August 2011?

On Tim Cahill

6   At which ground did Tim make his Everton debut in
    August 2004, the same venue where he had scored an
    FA Cup semi-final winner four months before?

7 At which club's ground did Tim famously score 4 goals in four separate matches, all headers and all at the same end?

8 How many Merseyside derby league goals did Tim score – the most by an Everton player in the post-war era?

9 Against which club, in January 2005 and March 2012, did the Australian score his first and last FA Cup goals for us?

10 To which club did Cahill head after leaving Everton in the summer of 2012?

On both

11 Both players scored injury-time goals as we came back from 3–1 down to memorably draw 3–3 against which team at Goodison in September 2010?

Round

24

Capital Quiz

The Toffees have enjoyed mixed fortunes in London, but here are a few questions to test your knowledge of our capital gains and losses.

1   Against which London side did Leighton Baines once score from two free-kicks in the same game?
2   But the England international was not the first Everton player to achieve this feat, Kevin Sheedy being the first to do so during a 3–2 league defeat at which London club in October 1986?
3   Against which London club did Everton lose nine successive away games between 1967 and 2008?

4   Who scored our winning spot-kick in the FA Cup
    penalty shoot-out at Stamford Bridge in February 2011
    after a 1–1 draw?
5   Which Spurs player scored a hat-trick in their 4–3
    victory over Everton in January 2003?
6   Everton last won a Premier League game at Arsenal in
    January 1996. Who scored the winner in a 2–1 victory
    for us?
7   Everton's bid for a fourth successive FA Cup final
    appearance disappeared in February 1987. Which side
    defeated the Toffees 3–1 at the fifth round stage in the
    capital?

8   Who was the unfortunate Everton goalkeeper who
    conceded seven times in the 7–0 loss at Arsenal in May
    2005 immediately after we had secured fourth place
    and a route to the Champions League?

9   Which club stalwart, in an unfamiliar midfield role on
    debut, won a penalty after being pole-axed by Stuart
    Pearce at Upton Park in March 2001?

10 Which lower league club knocked the Toffees out of
    the League Cup on penalties in the capital in September
    2010?

11 Which overseas player scored just 18 seconds after
    coming on as a substitute for us at Stamford Bridge in a
    Premier League game in October 2011?

Sticky Toffees Stuff

This round features unlucky keepers, shoelaces and a future Everton player who made Champions League history …

1   Who became the first opposition goalkeeper to concede 2 own goals in his career against Everton, during a Premier League game at Goodison in August 2016?

2   In winning his 40th cap at the club in 2016, who did Phil Jagielka replace as the player with the most England appearances whilst at Everton?

3   Who is the only Everton goalkeeper to have also appeared against the Toffees at Wembley?

4   Who was the first Everton player to appear for the club under five different permanent managers?

5   'It was because I've seen a foul made by another player,' were the words of which man about what?

6   In June 2015, an international featured five Everton players for the first time – who were the two countries involved?

7   Which full-back in 1981 was the last Everton player sold to Manchester United before Wayne Rooney more than two decades later?

8   Which future Everton player scored the first ever Champions League goal in 1992, when playing for Bruges?

9   In the 1986/87 season, who scored just 3 league goals but netted 8 times in the two major domestic cup competitions, a total which has not been exceeded since?

10 Who in 2010/11 was Everton's joint leading scorer in all competitions, in his only full season with the club?

11 Which Everton player was infamously tying his shoelaces in the penalty area as a Charlton equaliser sped past him at the Valley in November 2006?

Late 1980s and Beyond

These questions spans those years after our 1987 title-triumph to the dawn of the new Millennium, plenty to mull over from the eras of power dressing and Britpop.

1 Who left Everton to join Cardiff City in 1993, after joining the club as an apprentice more than sixteen years before?
2 Whose only hat-trick for the Toffees was in a 3–0 home victory over Coventry City in September 1991?
3 To which Italian club did Everton sell Andrei Kanchelskis for £8 million in January 1997?

4   Everton played in the game with the lowest ever
     top-flight gate in January 1993, but who were our
     opponents in front of just 3,039 spectators?

5   Which then lower division side took Everton to three
     games in the FA Cup fourth round in 1987/88, and then
     did the same in the third round two years later?

6   In December 1988 who successfully converted
     Everton's only penalty awarded at Anfield in the past
     eighty years?

7   Whose move to Arsenal for £2 million in February
     1993 was for the highest fee Everton had received from
     an English club for a player at the time?

8   Who set a club record for scoring the most penalties
     when netting his 19th spot-kick against Charlton at
     Goodison in April 1988?

9 Which lower division club shocked Everton with a
   3–2 FA Cup third-round replay victory at Goodison in
   January 1994?

10 'I played a one-two on the edge of the box with Tony
   Cottee and when it came back I lunged at it with a
   defender.' Who is the Everton player describing a
   famous goal?

11 Who was Everton's top scorer in the 1994/95 campaign
   with 16 goals in all competitions?

Round

27

Everton in Europe

Passports needed for this round as we head off to the Continent for some testers on our European adventures.

1   In 2014/15 Everton faced a French team for the first time. Who were our Gallic opponents in the Europa League group stages?

2   In that season's competition, we took our all-time record against which country to nine games played in European competitions without a single defeat?

3   Everton's first European Cup campaign in 1963/64 ended unluckily at the first hurdle when they lost 1–0 on aggregate to which Italian club?

4   Who is Everton's all-time top scorer in European games?

5   At Goodison in September 2014 Wolfsburg's Ricardo Rodriguez became only the fourth opposition player to achieve what feat in any Everton game?

6   One of our substitutes in the 1985 Cup Winners' Cup final was the only survivor in the squad from the previous European campaign in 1979/80, who was he?

7   Which winger was the only player to score for Everton in all three major European competitions?

8 Who made his only Everton appearance as a substitute against FC BATE Borisov in December 2009 and was later transferred for a reported fee of more than £35 million in 2016?

9 Who has made the most appearances for Everton in European competitions – 28 in total?

10 Which player in 2007/08 made history by playing against Everton in Europe and in the Merseyside derby during the same season – appearing for FC Zenit Saint Petersburg in December and at Anfield three months later?

11 Who scored his final Everton goal in the 2–0 second leg UEFA Cup victory over Fiorentina in March 2008?

Round
28

Blue Connections

For each of these questions there is a common theme – some perhaps more obvious than others. Get your Blue matter going with these testers.

1 1980s goalkeeper Bobby Mimms, defensive hard man Pat van den Hauwe, and midfielder Steven Pienaar – what is the common theme?

2 Everton great Alan Ball, defensive stalwart Dave Watson and midfielder Dan Gosling?

3 Midfielder Stuart McCall, Swedish international Niclas Alexandersson and 'Feed the Yak' Yakubu Aiyegbeni?

4 Leighton Baines, Phil Neville, James Vaughan and Phil Jagielka?

5 Andy van der Meyde, Steven Pienaar and Ramiro Funes Mori?

6 Swindon Town (1994), West Ham United (1999), Sunderland (2007)?

7 Midfielder Vinny Samways, stylish striker Louis Saha and flash-in-the-pan forward Nikica Jelavić?

8 Manchester United, Southampton and Tottenham Hotspur?

9 Peerless left-back Ray Wilson, centre-half Slaven Bilić and cult hero John Heitinga?

10 BBC *Match of the Day* host Gary Lineker, 1980s title-winner Adrian Heath and Israeli international Idan Tal?

11 Middlesbrough (0–3), Chelsea (1–2), Sunderland (0–3)?

Round
29

The Final Bag of Toffees

Here is the final bag of treats, enjoy them while they last!

1   Where did Andy Gray score a memorable winning goal
    described by Howard Kendall thus: 'Andy rotivated the
    ground with his nose as he slid in to meet the ball'?
2   Who is the only Everton player substituted more than
    100 times in his Goodison career, in 357 starts?
3   Who scored just 6 minutes into his Everton debut
    against Chelsea in August 2014?

4   Alan Shearer and which fellow England international forward have scored a record 16 Premier League goals against Everton?

5   Who is the only Italian to make 100 or more Premier League appearances for the Toffees?

6   In 2012 who took just 910 minutes playing time to score his first 10 goals for Everton, the fastest for us in 100 years?

7   Which team did Romelu Lukaku score against for a club-record ninth successive game in October 2016?

8   In March 2017, Morgan Schneiderlin became the first Everton player wearing the number 2 shirt to score since whom fourteen years previously?

9   Which former Everton player got a round of applause from the home crowd after scoring against the Toffees at Goodison in September 2016?

10 Who is Everton's most capped overseas outfield player – winning 55 caps when at Goodison?

11 Which player in the 1988/89 season scored his first 4 career goals for Everton all in domestic cup competitions?

Howard Kendall: The 1980s Management Years

As a wonderful player and a brilliantly successful manager, Howard Kendall is the single greatest figure in modern Everton history. It seems appropriate therefore that the final round of this book should be on his most memorable period – the trophy-laden years of the mid-1980s. I hope you have enjoyed the questions, and remember *Nil satis nisi optimum* (Only the best is good enough).

1 Which club did Howard manage before coming to Goodison in the summer of 1981?

2 Howard said, 'I can't say anything, I'm a hush puppy!' after which legendary manager described him as a 'young pup' in 1984?

3 Who did Howard sign for a fee of £840,000 in January 1987, a player who then faced his brother on his debut against Sheffield Wednesday?

4 Which key player's signing at Goodison in November 1983 was discovered only when a supporter told the *Liverpool Echo* that he had just been seen in a newsagent's shop by the ground?

5   Who scored our crucial second goal in the famous 2–1
     win at Spurs in April 1985 that effectively decided the
     title?

6   Everton went top of the table in April 1987 after which
     player's memorable late strike brought a 2–1 victory at
     Chelsea?

7   'That's how much they want you to win. If you can't
     do it for them today you'll never do it for anybody' –
     famous words from Howard, but where and when?

8   Which midfielder did Howard drop for the crucial
     league game at Spurs in April 1985, after scoring both
     goals in the crucial 2–1 win at Southampton four days
     before?

9   Howard's final game as a player with Everton in January 1982 was in the FA Cup. Who were the opponents, the same team he had faced when becoming the youngest cup finalist at Wembley eighteen years before?

10 Who did Howard describe as Everton's 'first million pound player' after signing him for a club record fee of £700,000 in January 1982?

11 Which team did Everton defeat 3–1 at Goodison in May 1987, on the day we received the league championship trophy?

1 Anfield.
2 Walter Smith.
3 Chelsea.
4 Tim Howard.
5 Three (as a player in 1969/70 and as a manager in 1984/85 and 1986/87).
6 Neville Southall – the great man making a record 751 appearances.
7 Colin Harvey, in the period 1987–1990.
8 Duncan Ferguson.
9 Phil Jagielka.
10 Bellefield.
11 Marouane Fellaini.

Under Martinez: Part 1

1 Ross Barkley.
2 Steven Pienaar.
3 Stevenage.
4 Kevin Mirallas.
5 James McCarthy.
6 Bournemouth. The Toffees went 3–2 ahead after 95 minutes only for the home team to equalise 3 minutes later.
7 Aiden McGeady.
8 Samuel Eto'o, who unusually chose to wear a shirt associated with a centre-half. The previous instance was Derek Mountfield v. Watford in 1986.
9 Dynamo Kiev.
10 Marouane Fellaini, for Manchester United.
11 Brendan Galloway.

Opening Days

1 Peter Beagrie.
2 Watford; the 1982/83 fixture was their first ever in the top-flight.
3 Arsenal in a 6–1 victory.
4 John Collins.
5 2–2. It was only the second time that three successive Everton opening-day fixtures had the same score, the first time was 1896–1898, when we won 2–1 in each season.
6 Andy Johnson.
7 Kevin Richardson, who then moved to Arsenal, where he won another championship-winner's medal in dramatic circumstances at Anfield in 1989.
8 Aiden McGeady.
9 Justin Fashanu (Norwich City) and John Fashanu (Aston Villa).
10 Manchester United, winning 1–0.
11 Richard Wright.

Round 4

A Mixed Bag of Toffees

1 Trevor Steven.

2 Ibrahima Bakayoko.

3 Mike Newell.

4 Lucas Neill, in a very short-lived spell.

5 Tony Hibbert, from 2000/01 to 2015/16 inclusive. Neville Southall went one better, playing in 17 campaigns.

6 Kevin Sheedy, many of them crackers, too.

7 Manchester United, the Scot scoring 12 goals in all.

8 Swansea City.

9 Gareth Farrelly – the second was the more famous goal against Coventry that secured top-flight safety in May 1998.

10 Villa Park – seven times in all.

11 David Lawson.

Round 5 **Toffees in the FA Cup**

1 West Ham United, who won 9–8 on penalties.
2 John Heitinga. Strangely, the defender only scored 2 league goals.
3 Oldham Athletic.
4 Liverpool.
5 Gordon Lee – the 11th was a 2–2 draw with Manchester City in March 1981, Everton lost the replay and Lee was sacked in the summer.
6 Kevin Ratcliffe.
7 Pat van den Hauwe.
8 David Unsworth.
9 Andy Gray after his controversial goal in the 1984 FA Cup final win against Watford, some claiming he headed the ball out of the goalkeeper's hands.
10 Tim Cahill, as it was his former club.
11 Blackburn Rovers.

Round 6 **Goodison Goings-On**

1 The first goal awarded after the use of goal-line technology on the ground.

2 It was the famous game where West Ham's Paolo Di Canio picked up the ball, when the Italian had a chance to score, so that stricken Everton goalkeeper Paul Gerrard could receive treatment.

3 A spectator bizarrely handcuffed himself to the goalpost at the Park End.

4 Aston Villa.

5 Graham Poll.

6 Norwich City, the last penalty shoot-out victory had been against Borussia Mönchengladbach in 1970.

7 Southampton (8–0 in 1971, 6–1 in 1986, 7–1 in 1996).

8 Referee Peter Walton left his red and yellow cards in the dressing room, and when cautioning Birmingham's Jordon Mutch in the opening period brandished an imaginary yellow card! Thankfully he retrieved the cards for the second half.

9 Leon Osman after a great run by Leighton Baines and a clever back-heel from Steve Pienaar.

10 Sylvester Stallone. The Rocky star attended as a guest of then Everton shareholder Robert Earl.

11 After the famous 1–0 win over Liverpool in October 1978, these words came from the policeman who said 'Get off the pitch' when BBC reporter Richard Duckenfield attempted to interview match-winner Andy King pitch-side after the game – the bobby then famously pushed both men onto the side-lines.

Premier League: The Noughties and Beyond

1 West Ham United.
2 Steven Pienaar – Sir Alex Ferguson later said this goal cost them the title, as they lost it on goal difference to Manchester City.
3 Denis Stracqualursi.
4 Newcastle United.
5 Phil Jagielka.
6 Manchester United – thanks to Bryan Oviedo's late goal.
7 Fulham – a perfect treble too: left-foot, right-foot and a header.
8 Louis Saha.
9 Leighton Baines. At the time only five other players had achieved the feat twice.
10 Romelu Lukaku at Sunderland in September 2016, in just 11 minutes – the second fastest in the post-war era after Bob Latchford's 10-minute treble against Crystal Palace in 1980.
11 Joseph Yobo.

Round 8 — Loan Stars

1 Manuel Fernandes – the Portuguese player scoring 2 goals in 24 games.
2 Matteo Ferrari.
3 Philippe Senderos – the defender playing just three times.
4 Brian McBride – from Columbus Crew in 2003.
5 Ian Durrant, although his playing shirt originally said 'Durant'.
6 Thomas Gravesen.
7 Royston Drenthe in 2011/12.
8 Christian Atsu.
9 Eric Dier – the player returning to Portugal at the end of the 2011/12 season.
10 In Turkey with Trabzonspor.
11 Landon Donovan.

Blues Opponents

Round 9

1. Sunderland – 6–2 in November 2015.
2. Arsenal – the Gunners achieving their 100th victory in March 2015, best keep quiet about it though!
3. Newcastle United – 1–0 away and 3–0 at home.
4. Chelsea, including an FA Cup final and a League Cup semi-final.
5. Bristol Rovers (lost in 2000/01) and Bristol City (won in 2004/05).
6. Leeds United – our previous league victory had been in the second division, so it was actually our first top-flight win at Elland Road since February 1939.
7. Tony Pulis, with Stoke (2011/12), Crystal Palace (2013/14) and West Brom (2015/16).
8. Selhurst Park (Crystal Palace), including four successive clean sheets from 2013/14 to 2016/17. The record is 500 minutes at Anfield from 1906 to 1912.
9. West Ham United.
10. Southampton.
11. Leeds United, the Toffees succeeding the Yorkshire team as champions in 1969/70.

Another Mixed Bag of Toffees

1 Peter Beardsley, at a bargain £1 million in the summer of 1991.

2 Arsenal.

3 Graeme Sharp, including the famous winner at the Anfield Road end in October 1984.

4 Gary Naysmith, with an injury time goal in the 3–0 win over Portsmouth.

5 Neville Southall after his memorable late save from Spurs' Mark Falco in the crucial 2–1 win at White Hart Lane in April 1985.

6 Trevor Steven, who came in for Alan Irvine. Andy Gray had replaced Kevin Sheedy.

7 Simon Davies.

8 John Stones.

9 Blackpool. Gordon West came for a record fee of £27,000 in 1962, George Wood for £150,000 in 1977.

10 Monday.

11 Leandro Rodriguez, the Uruguayan forward.

The Merseyside Derby

Round 11

1. Tim Howard – from Dirk Kuyt at Goodison in October 2011.
2. Maurice Johnston, in a 1–1 draw and a 2–1 victory respectively.
3. David Weir.
4. Senegal – Everton's Idrissa Gueye facing Liverpool's Sadio Mane.
5. David Burrows.
6. Sami Hyypia, the game infamous for what Everton supporters thought was a contentious display by referee Mark Clattenburg.
7. Richard Dunne.
8. Francis Jeffers, who scored in the 3–2 defeat in April 1999 and was sent off for brawling with Liverpool keeper Sander Westerveld five months later.
9. Steve McMahon.
10. Joel Robles, at Goodison in December 2016 for the injured Maarten Stekelenburg.
11. Belgium – Kevin Mirallas and Romelu Lukaku in the 3–3 draw at Goodison in November 2013.

Overseas Blues

1 Tim Cahill, who scored 68 goals.
2 Louis Saha, who won his only cap at Goodison in 2010.
3 Lacina Traoré, who was on loan from Monaco and was injured for a lengthy spell.
4 Shani Tarashaj, who played for Switzerland whilst on loan at Grasshoppers.
5 Tomasz Radzinski, who later moved to Canada, for whom he played international football.
6 Jan Mucha, who had limited opportunities thanks to Tim Howard's ever-present record.
7 Thomas Gravesen, for Denmark.
8 Sunderland, Magaye in April 2012 and Idrissa in February 2017.
9 Norway – Thomas Myhre and Espen Baardsen (the latter was born in the USA but qualified for the Scandinavian country).
10 Sylvain Distin, in 2014.
11 Abel Xavier in 2001/02, for Everton in the September and, after moving mid-season, for Liverpool in the February.

Debuts to Remember (and Forget!)

1 Kevin Richardson.
2 Carlo Nash.
3 David Johnson, who also scored on his youth team and reserve debuts. The striker was sold to Ipswich in 1972 and then moved to Anfield four years later.
4 Gary Speed.
5 Glenn Keeley, who was on loan from Blackburn at the time.
6 Dominic Calvert-Lewin. The final minute of the game featured both goalkeepers in the Everton goal at the same time as Arsenal pressed for an equaliser!
7 Neil Pointon, known to supporters as 'Dissa'.
8 Muhamed Bešić. The injury-plagued midfielder then limped out of the same fixture after just 9 minutes in the following season.
9 Iain Turner, after Wright infamously injured himself before the game in an area where warming up was prohibited.
10 Paul Power, with the veteran going on to be a title-winner.
11 Ademola Lookman. The fastest is Tony Cottee's 30-second strike against Newcastle in August 1988.

1 Billy Bingham.
2 February 1974.
3 Wimbledon, Martin Dobson netting a hat-trick too.
4 Andy King, in both games of the 1978/79 season and in October 1979.
5 The floodlights failed, stopping the game temporarily. The other occasion had been at Goodison Park against Manchester United in December 1975.
6 Mick Lyons, the club skipper.
7 Ken McNaught, who moved to Aston Villa in the summer.
8 Joe Harper.
9 Brian Labone; the last of 534 appearances for the man Harry Catterick called the 'Last of the Corinthians'.
10 Duncan McKenzie, who could famously jump over a Mini and throw a golf ball the length of a pitch.
11 Manchester United.

Comeback Kings

1 Barnsley.

2 West Brom, the previous occurrence had been a 4–3 victory at Ipswich in November 1985.

3 Tomasz Radzinski.

4 Peter Beardsley, in a 2–1 victory.

5 Romelu Lukaku.

6 Blackpool. The Toffees were leading 1–0 and 2–1, then trailed 3–2 before emerging victorious.

7 BSC Young Boys of Berne.

8 Gareth Barry.

9 Bayern Munich, famously in the 3–1 semi-final win at Goodison.

10 Thomas Gravesen.

11 Leon Osman.

Toffees for the Three Lions

1 Jack Rodwell.
2 Phil Jagielka, in the 2010 and 2014 qualifiers.
3 David Unsworth.
4 Michael Ball – with Alan Ball the only two players capped by England in the post-war era with the same surname.
5 John Stones.
6 Nick Barmby – also the only player capped for England at both Everton and Liverpool.
7 Trevor Steven. The previous player had been Bob Latchford in 1979.
8 Gary Lineker – including a famous World Cup hat-trick against Poland in 1986.
9 Andy Hinchcliffe.
10 Dave Watson.
11 Andy Johnson.

Round 17 Howard Kendall: The 1990s Management Years

1 Woking.
2 Crystal Palace.
3 Sheffield United – Howard Kendall also lead them out at Wembley in the play-offs in 1997.
4 Matt Jackson.
5 Maurice Johnston.
6 Don Hutchison.
7 Peter Beardsley.
8 Mark Ward.
9 Maine Road, the Manchester City fans still not happy about his departure to Everton three years before.
10 Michael Ball and Danny Cadamarteri.
11 David Unsworth.

Under Martinez: Part II

1 Gareth Barry, who played for Aston Villa when they beat Chelsea 2–0 in September 2007.

2 Sunderland.

3 Nikica Jelavić. The other player was Jock Dodds against Chelsea in April 1947.

4 Arouna Koné.

5 Ramiro Funes Mori.

6 Seamus Coleman.

7 Steven Naismith.

8 Kevin Mirallas.

9 Leicester City.

10 Shane Duffy.

11 Phil Jagielka.

Round 19 Tell Me Ma, Me Ma ... We're Going to Wembley

1 Romelu Lukaku – in the 2016 FA Cup semi-final against Manchester United, and it was saved by David de Gea.

2 Andy Gray – for Aston Villa in the 1977 League Cup final, and for the Toffees in the 1984 FA Cup final.

3 Joseph Yobo.

4 Paul Scholes.

5 Mike Lyons.

6 Gary Lineker.

7 Kevin Ratcliffe. Neville Southall and Graeme Sharp both made 10 in total.

8 Graeme Sharp, in the 1984 FA Cup final and the 1989 Simod Cup final against Nottingham Forest.

9 Mike Newell.

10 Jack Rodwell.

11 Chris Smalling, playing for Manchester United in the 2016 FA Cup semi-final at Wembley. Curiously, this was his second own goal against us; the first was for Fulham at Goodison in April 2010.

The Early Bath

1 Don Hutchison.
2 Kevin Mirallas.
3 David Unsworth; Marco Materazzi had been the first sent off on the ground three times, but these were all in different competitions.
4 Tim Cahill, on scoring his first goal for the club.
5 Gareth Barry.
6 Chelsea.
7 Neville Southall.
8 David Weir.
9 Phil Neville.
10 Jack Rodwell.
11 Vinnie Jones.

Round 21 — Yet Another Mixed Bag of Toffees

1 Kenny Sansom, the full-back.
2 Steven Naismith, including a hat-trick in September 2015 at Goodison.
3 Andy King, the chirpy southerner who sadly died in 2015.
4 Tony Cottee.
5 Tomasz Radzinski.
6 Seamus Coleman – the Irishman netting 19 goals from right-back (24 overall).
7 Victor Anichebe, who scored 25 times.
8 Mark and Stephen Hughes.
9 Kevin Campbell.
10 The great Alex Young, dubbed 'the Golden Vision'.
11 Phil Jagielka.

Wearing the Armband

1 Leighton Baines.

2 Leon Osman.

3 Steven Pienaar.

4 Mark Higgins. The defender initially retired through injury in 1984 before making a comeback with Manchester United.

5 Slaven Bilić.

6 Dave Watson.

7 Duncan Ferguson v. Bolton in December 1997.

8 David Weir.

9 Ross Barkley who, at 22 years 8 months, was the youngest since Steve McMahon in 1983.

10 Seamus Coleman.

11 John Collins.

Round 23 **Blues Brothers in Arms**

1. Real Sociedad.
2. Crystal Palace.
3. Newcastle (St James Park).
4. Hull City.
5. Blackburn Rovers, after the home team had missed two spot-kicks themselves.
6. Old Trafford, in a goal-less draw against Manchester United. The Australian had scored the winner there for Millwall in an FA Cup semi-final against Sunderland in April 2004.
7. Manchester City. The Toffees won all four games too.
8. Five goals in total. Only four Everton players have scored more in the league derby.
9. Sunderland, in a 3–0 win and a 1–1 draw.
10. New York Red Bulls.
11. Manchester United.

Capital Quiz

1 West Ham United, in September 2013.
2 Charlton Athletic.
3 Fulham.
4 Phil Neville.
5 Robbie Keane, in what was Espen Baardsen's only game as Everton keeper.
6 Andrei Kanchelskis.
7 Wimbledon, after Everton were leading 1–0 as well.
8 Richard Wright. It was rumoured that the players had allegedly partied hard in celebration three days before!
9 Tony Hibbert.
10 Brentford.
11 Apostolos Vellios.

Sticky Toffees Stuff

1 Shay Given. The other own goal for the Irishman had been at Newcastle in October 2007.

2 Alan Ball.

3 Nigel Martyn, in the 1991 ZDS Cup final for Crystal Palace.

4 Dave Watson – under Howard Kendall, Colin Harvey, Mike Walker, Joe Royle and Walter Smith.

5 Pierluigi Collina, talking about Duncan Ferguson's infamous disallowed goal at Villarreal in the Champions League qualifier in August 2005. The Italian, in his final game as a referee, claimed it was a result of a foul committed by Marcus Bent, who looked more sinned against than sinner.

6 England and the Republic of Ireland. Seamus Coleman, James McCarthy, Aiden McGeady, Ross Barkley and Phil Jagielka were the players, although not all were on the pitch simultaneously.

7 John Gidman.

8 Daniel Amokachi.

9 Paul Wilkinson, seven in the League Cup and one in the FA Cup.

10 Jermaine Beckford.

11 Joseph Yobo – only the Nigerian knows why!

Late 1980s
and Beyond

1 Kevin Ratcliffe.
2 Peter Beardsley.
3 Fiorentina.
4 Wimbledon, the Toffees winning 3–1.
5 Middlesbrough.
6 Wayne Clarke, who also had a goal controversially disallowed in the game.
7 Martin Keown.
8 Trevor Steven, overtaking the great Roy Vernon, who missed just one of the nineteen penalties he had taken.
9 Bolton Wanderers.
10 Graham Stuart, on the winner against Wimbledon in 1994 that kept Everton in the top-flight.
11 Paul Rideout, the most famous goal coming in the FA Cup final.

Everton in Europe

1 Lille, the Toffees drawing 1–1 in France and winning 3–0 at Goodison.

2 Germany, having beaten Wolfsburg twice in 2014/15.

3 Inter Milan, who went on to lift the trophy.

4 Romelu Lukaku, with 8 goals.

5 The defender scored at both ends of the pitch.

6 John Bailey.

7 Johnny Morrissey in the European Cup, Fairs (UEFA) Cup and Cup Winners' Cup.

8 Shkodran Mustafi, who joined Arsenal from Valencia in 2016, having left Goodison for Sampdoria in 2012.

9 Tim Howard.

10 Martin Škrtel, who left for Anfield in the January 2008 transfer window.

11 Andy Johnson.

1 All were sold to Tottenham Hotspur.

2 They all scored the winning goals against Liverpool in FA Cup games. Ball (1967), Watson (1991) and Gosling in 2009 (unless you were one of the unfortunate viewers who saw an advert on ITV instead).

3 They have all scored goals at the World Cup whilst at Everton. McCall for Scotland in 1990, Alexandersson (against England) in 2002 and the Yak for Nigeria in 2010.

4 They all scored penalties in our 4–2 shoot-out win over Manchester United at Wembley in the 2009 FA Cup semi-final.

5 They are the last three Everton players to be sent off at Anfield in Merseyside derbies.

6 Games at Goodison where we have scored 6 goals or more in the Premier League – Swindon (6–2), West Ham (6–0), Sunderland (7–1).

7 The last three Everton players to score at Wembley.

8 The clubs beaten by the Toffees at the semi-final stage on the last three occasions we have won the FA Cup – Manchester United (1966), Southampton (1984) and Spurs (1995).

9 They have appeared in World Cup semi-finals when at Everton: Wilson (England, 1966), Bilić (Croatia, 1998) and Heitinga (Holland, 2010).

10 All three moved to Spanish clubs: Lineker (Barcelona, 1986), Heath (Espanol, 1988) and Tal (Rayo Vallecano, 2002).

11 The final games of the three Everton managers prior to Ronald Koeman: Walter Smith, David Moyes and Roberto Martinez.

Round 29 The Final Bag of Toffees

1 Against Notts County in a 2–1 victory at Meadow Lane in the FA Cup quarter-final in 1984. The Scot netted the winning goal with a diving header as he slid along the ground.

2 Leon Osman.

3 Samuel Eto'o.

4 Les Ferdinand (QPR, Newcastle, Spurs, Leicester).

5 Alessandro Pistone, 103 from 2000 to 2005.

6 Nikica Jelavić.

7 West Ham United.

8 Steve Watson with his hat-trick goal against Leeds United in September 2003, although the Geordie was playing midfield on the day. Tony Hibbert took over the number 2 shirt in 2005/06 and failed to give us a chance to riot!

9 Steven Naismith, for Norwich City in the League Cup.

10 Joseph Yobo, for Nigeria.

11 Stuart McCall.

Round 30 Howard Kendall: The 1980s Management Years

1 Blackburn Rovers.
2 Brian Clough, after a 5–0 win for Everton in December 1984.
3 Ian Snodin, who faced brother Glynn.
4 Andy Gray.
5 Trevor Steven, who memorably dribbled past Ray Clemence before slotting home.
6 Alan Harper, from all of 30 yards.
7 At Stoke City, before the third round FA Cup tie in 1984. Everton won 2–0 and went on to lift the trophy.
8 Kevin Richardson.
9 West Ham United.
10 Adrian Heath.
11 Luton Town.